TABLE OF CONTENTS

GARMENT OF WORSHIP

INTRODUCTION 3

CHAPTER 1 7
Vessel Chosen

CHAPTER 2 31
The Garment in the Making

CHAPTER 3 49
Garment fit for the Master's Use

CHAPTER 4 72
Reachable

CHAPTER 5 87
Spiritual Maintenance

CHAPTER 6 96
Benefits of Obedience

LESLIE'S BIO

GARMENT OF WORSHIP

Lord I thank you for what you have planned for my life without hesitation or wavering. The countless blessings and the promises of your word increases my faith daily. Lord I thank you for your hand of mercy and grace that supersedes all my expectation. Great is thy faithfulness morning by morning new mercy I see... Thank you for creating me to be used for your glory; and teaching me through your word. Praying, fasting, believing and presenting my body as a living sacrifice, holy and acceptable unto God.

In loving memory of Mother Catherine Nesbitt…
For her obedience to God's will and assignment
to witness and take me to church…… Because of
you, my life changed forever.

VESSEL CHOSEN

INTRODUCTION

Have you ever had a dream so beautiful, seem so real, but when you woke up, you realize that it was not real, you were sound asleep? We all have a purpose. He has a promise for all of us and it is not a dream. Although the road we travel to our destination has some road conditions, detours, we got to keep pushing and keep driving until we reach that place. When I realize that I was chosen, I was so excited to know that the Lord found favor in me, and I thank him for designing me as a vessel and giving me an assignment. Also, with each assignment, come instructions for the next level, and the next level, and the next level and it keeps going. As a believer, I have to continue to pray for his love, his protection, his approval and his validation. Daily he was molding me to become a garment of worship for his glory. God has called me to be a steward of what he has planned for my life, not just to be a reader and doer of the word but spreading the gospel to others as well.

GARMENT
(GAHR-MUHNT)

Noun
1) any article of clothing:*dresses, suits, and other garments.*
2) an outer covering or outward appearance.

Verb (used with object)
1) to clothe, dress, or cover.

WORSHIP
(WUR-SHIP)

Noun
1) reverent honor and homage paid to God or a sacred personage, or to any object regarded as sacred.
2) formal or ceremonious rendering of such honor and homage:*They attended worship this morning.*

Verb (used with object), **wor·shiped, wor·ship·ing** or (*especially British*) **wor·shipped, wor·ship·ping.**
1) to render religious reverence and homage to.
2) to feel an adoring reverence or regard for (any person or thing).

Definitions: 'Dictionary.com'

Chapter 1

VESSEL CHOSEN

But ye are a chosen generation, a royal priesthood, an holy nation, a peculiar people; that ye should shew forth the praises of him who hath called you out of darkness into his marvelous light;
(1 Peter 2:9)

There are a lot of situations and experiences we face in life that can either escort us to victory or consequences we get because of wrong decisions. Life's experiences pave the way for our future. Whenever you make the decision to accept the Lord as your Savior, and you live faithfully to the end, there is a reward of eternal life. As a little girl, growing up in a small town was challenging. But something happened to me that ultimately changed my life forever. When I was a little girl, I spent a lot of time over my grandmother's house without knowing my playtime outside was about to get interrupted with something great. God planted a Missionary across the street that was about her father's business in ministry. While I was playing in the yard, Missionary Catherine Nesbitt walks across the street and asks my grandmother if she could take me to church; and the new normal began with my grandmother's response in just three words, "YES YOU CAN". Right then and there my new life began with the Lord and I didn't even know. I was unaware of what was about to take place in the next decades of my life. The will of the Lord was well activated and I did not have a clue, neither did I have the instruction manual in my hand. Missionary Nesbitt started taking me to the church and the experiences of those first services were very foreign to me. People singing, clapping, lifting their hands and praying to someone that they could not see, was so confusing. I kept going and it became more interesting. The adventure, the journey of finding out what those people were doing worshipping, praying, singing, shouting, praising this man, was beginning to be present in my life. They were doing all of this and I never saw this person who they call Lord, Healer, Deliverer, Provider but I was attracted to it. Sometimes you may not know the full details of why the Lord tells you to do something, but PLEASE OBEY HIM. You may not know every reason or detail behind it, but trust me; you will know it by and by. Mother Nesbitt kept taking me to the Services faithfully; Sunday School, YPWW, Bible Band, Home and Foreign Missions, Sunday Morning and Sunday Night Services and even though I didn't know everything clearly, but I began falling in love with the foundation of my new beginning. I was so happy about this new normal, and the congregation of people I was getting acquainted with and introduced to. These new experiences were already blessing my life, as I observed their faithfulness and eagerness to learn and live by his word. The beginning of my journey with the Lord all resulted from a Missionary taking me to church with a greasy brown bag full of black and white cookies to keep me from being hungry during services.

How to define and learn about the basics of life can only be found in the word of God. The bible declares in 2nd Timothy 2:15 "Study to show thyself approved unto god, a workman that needeth not to be ashamed, rightly dividing the word of truth". While learning how to read I was given and introduced to this book that I saw Mother Catherine Nesbitt caring called the Holy Bible. The more I read the word, the more I learned. When a person disciplines themselves to study the word of God, it enhances their faith. While spending so much time at my grandmother's house, shelling peas, canning peaches, stacking wood, and making pickles, I was not only learning survival skills naturally; I was also learning how to obtain knowledge for my spiritual assignment. I learned in the word that Jesus taught in many ways so we would understand and have clarity of his word. He taught in parables, with stones, and clay so people will understand his word clearly. The more I attended the services, the more I fell in love with the experiences, and the Word. The people at church were called Saints which I learned were people who we believed were holy. Wow! What a new word in my vocabulary. Saints, people who loved the Lord with their whole heart. It would blow my mind to see how dedicated and consistent they were in praying, fasting, worshipping, and encouraging others to hold on. The more I attended, and listened, the more I learned the details of the word. I could not read much of the word but I heard them read and they explained it to me. What I seen them do eventually become a part of who I was becoming, and yes I was falling in love with the church and finding out the purpose of my existence.

Didn't have very much growing up, but I knew something was happening on the inside of me that I really couldn't explain. I started realizing and learning that regardless of where I came from, who my family was or what I did not have, the Lord saw something in me that I could hardly see myself. I was learning my assignment at an incredibly young age and was developing an appetite to learn more and more about being a chosen vessel. You know what? Although I didn't know a lot about the Lord and his plans for my life, but my heart beat with enthusiasm. Knowing that God had his hands on my life THAT FEELING FELT GOOD.

"The more I read the word, the more I learned".

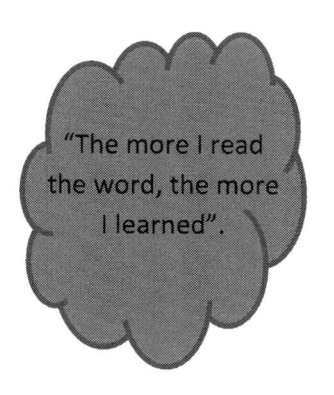

As I continue to grow and attend the church, the Saints started to see that this little country girl had worth that needed to be tilled and cultivated. Even though, I was very young, I started going consistently to church and learning more and more about the Lord. The Saints continued to embrace and pray for me, realizing that God chose me to do a work for him. They recognized the desire I had for more of God. I had to keep studying and attending the services because I wanted to love the Lord with all my heart and soul.

> My heart beat with enthusiasm knowing that God had me on his mind.

One day, I learned that Missionary Catherine Nesbitt who had been taking me to church passed and went home to be with the Lord. Then I thought, standing there outside of her house whose going to take me now, but thank the Lord, I lived close to the church and a lot of children were being picked up and I kept going. I am grateful to the Lord that she had faithfully taken me enough for me to catch on and continue to go. I also had to learn about the devil, Satan and his attacks. The devil wasn't far behind and at any time he would try to prevent me from fulfilling my God ordained assignment. The saints continued to pray and teach me how to stay on the Lord's side. Although, I was a little young girl, and didn't fully understand all that they had experienced in their lives, but whenever I saw them in church, at the store, or at home, they valued their relationship with the Lord. They loved the Lord so much that I didn't notice the attack of the enemy on their lives. When a person loves God, and really sincerely love him, it outweighs the attacks of the enemy in their lives. Their desire for God inspired me to keep going. They allowed their light to shine everywhere. They gave no credit to the devil. The bible says in James 4:7 "Submit yourselves therefore to God, resist the devil and he will flee from you". I was learning more about holiness and what the Lord wanted me to do. To hear the Saints testify about how God brought them through, brought them over and brought them out, brought so much joy to my hear. However, I wanted to know him personally and know that he was active and present in my life as well. When I was at the age of 12yrs old, I was in a church play. I was the only character and a portrait that they used as Jesus and a brother talking through the microphone. He quoted the scripture in the word that says: "Ye have not chosen me, but I have chosen you, and ordained you, that ye should go and bring forth fruit, and that your fruit should remain: that whatsoever ye shall ask of the Father in my name, he may give it you" (John 15:16).

While still trying to figure out my purpose and how to walk in it, I thank God for the little knowledge that I did know, and what he was doing in others. Even though I was not rich, neither had a silver spoon in my hand, I was yet determined to know why I was chosen by God. Although my family and friends didn't understand my life as a believer; I continued to have an appetite not just for the Word of God but for his presence and the anointing. The more I prayed the more he fed me his word and I got knowledge from it. He chose me, and he was molding and making me into what he created me to be even if that was yet to be discovered by me. I was becoming a GARMENT THAT WOULD WORSHIP HIM. I didn't even know if I was good enough to go and do the things of God. I was going to the altar many times when I thought I failed God. My appetite and desire for his presence continued to increase. I thought I was hungry naturally so, but it was a spiritual hunger and thirst for the love of God. Matthew 5:6 says: Blessed are they which do hunger and thirst after righteousness: for they shall be filled. Even though I did not fully understand the call of God on my life, I

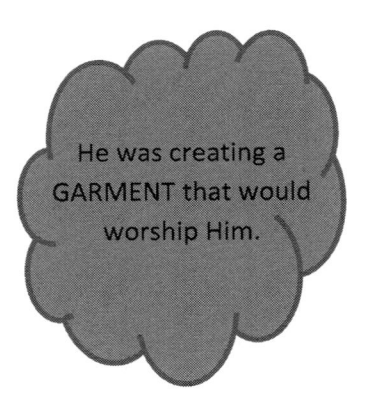

still was thirsty and hungry for more. Even though I knew very little about holiness something good was happening on the inside of my heart. I knew that if I held on to what I already knew God would keep me. This new normal was always in my mind.

> "Thou would keep him in perfect peace, whose mind is stayed on thee: because he trusted in thee".
> (Isaiah 26:3)

If we learn to keep our minds on him; He would lead and show us the way. Although I made many mistakes, fell-down, and had short comings, the love of the Lord lifted me up. When it seemed as though I couldn't take another step, the Lord was already there picking me up, pulling me through, giving me strength and forgiving me. Paul wrote in Romans 7:21 'I find then a law, that, when I would do good, evil is present with me, the one who wants to do good'. The Lord wants us to do good. Not only does he just appoint the assignments, but he walks with you and he talks with you all the way. He wants us to be blessed and to be a good steward of his word. I strive in life to be obedient and live for God. Lord, I thank you because you have never left me alone.

Satan is always present, always trying, always planning, and always plotting to hinder, to stop, and to discourage you from doing the will of the Lord. Some things that happen in our lives become comical to the devil because he tries daily to distract us from doing the will of the Lord. When we sincerely give our lives to the Lord, it is not only beneficial to us but to our family and those that are connected to us. No matter how far I drift, or have drifted, fell or have fallen, he forgave and comforted me with LOVE, JOY AND PEACE. People will sometimes change how they feel about you and may not forgive you completely but God; I thank you for not giving up on me!!!!! I learned that without the Lord, I was lost, up the creek without a paddle.

Yes, he was making me a GARMENT OF WORSHIP, a vessel that was willing to run and live for him. A garment that could stand and withstand in the days when it seems like all odds was against me. Knowing that life experiences would make the Garment (temple) stronger and more useful for his glory; which should be everyone's desire. For we were birthed from the Lord's mind, his hand, his creation. I was learning that his hands, that I couldn't see was holding, carrying, protecting, and embracing me daily.

I started going through some major things in my life at a very young age. I was the only one in my intermediate family that was trying to live this life of holiness. My family did not understand why I loved the church or the Lord so much, or why I started carrying this book called the bible and why my taste in music changed, even my dress code changed. I was learning that God had chosen me, and he was teaching and preparing me for an assignment ahead. When some people would ask me, what's going on with me, I didn't know how to explain to them the feeling I was having down on the inside because I did not clearly understand myself. The more I experienced different situations in life, the more I wanted to know how to get him to help me. I learned that even in the dark, the Lord was my light. Even in the dry places, the Lord was my river of life, even when my heart was hurting, he was my comforter. Lord, you are my strength and I thank you. The more I was attacked the more the garment was stained, torn, stretched by the obstacles, pulled by the enemy, attacked with trials, test, and tribulations of life, I knew the SEAMTRESS (THE LORD) WAS THERE IN THE SPIRIT SOWING, MENDING, and STITCHING IT BACK TOGETHER AGAIN. You must understand that everybody may not know your calling, but you must be confident. Keep striving and praying to get to a place in your relationship with God because he called you and not man. Philippians 1:6 says: Being confident of this very thing, that he which hath begun a good work in you will perform it until the day of Jesus Christ. Young and trying to find out more about God was sometimes a struggle because there were some people around me not interested in what I was experiencing. You have to stay focus and not get distracted by others that doubt the call on your life. My surroundings outside of the church weren't the same as at the church, so I was struggling trying to hold on to what I had experienced in the services, in Bible Class, Sunday school, and YPWW and so on. Even though, I was distracted many times, I still desired to learn more about the Lord. Sometimes we become distracted, listening and conforming to this World and not the Word. I was too young to realize that my grandmother's answer of yes activated my assignment, put into motion, and started the process to become a garment of Worship. The travel and the journey with the Lord were well on its way. He had me on his mind even before I learned of him and my purpose. At school my classmates teased me and laughed at me how I was dressed. I couldn't wait to get to church, even though I was being attacked, I still would testify about being saved and wanting to be the young lady that the Lord was calling for. Every time, I got up to testify I would sing the song, Lord, don't move my mountain but give me the strength to climb. The saints told me to be encouraged and hold on. The Saints would often say to me, 'daughter, THE LORD HAS A WORK FOR YOU TO DO'. Many times, I would get up and testify of the goodness of the Lord. I was glad to be saved and wanted more of him. The saints continued to embrace me and teach me wisdom. There were many times in my life that I ask the Lord, why me? I started praying about why I was chosen, why he picked me and why he began in me at such a young age. I realized that the more I loved the Lord, the more I felt his love for me, and I realized then that I was chosen to do something. I continued soul searching and word searching for the instructions to this journey with the Lord. The more I attended the services, I seen how the Lord healed, delivered, saved and reclaimed backsliders. I would be overwhelmed and filled with emotions in those Fire Revivals, but the more I experienced, the more I cried out to the Lord and the greater desire I had to learn of him. God was changing other people in those services, breaking bad habits, healing their sickness and blessing their children. The more you seek him the more you want to seek him. His presence can never be compared to anything you experience in your entire life. Ooh my Lord, I enjoyed being in the midst of Bible Believing, Faith Walkers, Prayer Warriors, dedicated people. I know they we're human and we made mistakes. I know that we are not perfect, and we error. However, I did not look for trips, errors or falls, I enjoyed seeing them praising and magnifying the Lord. They enjoyed coming to the house of the Lord, giving him the glory and the praise. As time went on, my appetite for holiness grew, it was my favorite meal and I began more and more latching on to those experiences and atmospheres. My craving for the Lord's presence in my life grew more. Although, I

> The more you seek him, the more, the more you want to seek him.

didn't understand my purpose fully, I didn't stop. Even when I had fallen short, those gospel songs, the preach word help me to discover the anchor I needed to have to hold on. God had already begun ordaining the works in me and the more I prayed for his presence, it was manifesting and revealing the new normal in my life.

At first, I couldn't picture the purpose, I couldn't frame his handiwork. What he was trying to show me seemed blurry. All I knew was that something was different, exciting, refreshing and I loved it. No, I couldn't fully understand what was going on in the inside, but I was being changed and the Lord had an agenda for my life. All I had to do was surrender and let him lead and carry me all the way. God created me, made me, my life cycle and he knew how to create the garment that would glorify him. Even though, I was learning more about the Lord, I felt things trying to attack me. Satan had tricks, weapons and barriers that tried to hinder me from learning and doing what the Lord said do. Satan tried to make me feel incapable of being a vessel chosen for the master's use. That is why you have to stay busy, keep running and moving forward. Always remember that an idle mind is the devil's workshop, so the Saints involved me as much as they could in the church. They encouraged me and pushed me toward the Lord's word. I was in pigtails, had very few skirts or dresses, but I had a yearning and a burning desire for the Lord. I knew that he was with me and would never leave me nor forsake me. Oh, I had a heavenly deposit in my heart, I was learning about the one that could and would supply all my needs according to his riches in glory. My temple is the garment that the Holy Ghost dwells in. 'For in this we groan, earnestly desiring to be clothed upon with our house which is from heaven: If so be that being clothed we shall not be found naked" (2nd Corinthians 5:2-3).

Chapter 2

GARMENT IN THE MAKING

Even everyone that is called by my name: for I have created him for my glory, I have formed him; yea, I have made him.
(Isaiah 43:7)

I heard someone say, into each life, some rain must fall, but after the rain the sun will shine. I live with anticipation knowing that there is a God given assignment on my life. I was young and had to recognize God's voice, which was a process. Being the only one saved in my home, I had to get all the knowledge from the church services and from the encouragement of the saints. Studying, reading and believing in the word required focus and learning how to trust a God that I never seen before. I was so eager to learn more about him. There were times after leaving the services, I would go home, for hours I would sit in the rocking chair in front of the radio with my bible, reading and learning about God's word and what I had experienced at the church. It's a beautiful thing to know that you're chosen. Many people are excited about being chosen by others, but it is more precious to be chosen by the Lord.

It's also a blessing to find out and know that you are created for his glory. However, knowing and doing are two different things. Some things in life are easier said than done. It does not matter who you are, how much you have in the bank, or who family you are associated with, some people don't favor you. Be mindful when the Lord has a calling on your life, everybody not going to believe in you or pat you on your back, they are not even going to forget your old ways and accept your change. Everybody is not going to receive what you say, but you got to keep going and keep growing. The more I allowed the Lord to mode and make me, the more people had their own opinion of what they thought I should be doing with my life. Let me not forget Satan on my back, trying to stop me constantly. Some people refuse to believe that I had a God given gift and was saved. Some thought it didn't take going to church all the time to be pleasing in the Lord's eyesight. I had to realize that you will never get everybody to like you. Everybody not going to agree, encourage or believe in you. You got to know who validates you. Some people are not going to understand your calling or what you are doing, but continue to stay focused and put your entire trust in the Lord. Keep pressing and stay on track. Some people want you to give up and give in, but keep running you will win. In the midst of those accusations, God continued what he begun in me.

The start of life's journey requires that your garment (your temple) be weather resistant and be able to withstand whatever storm you encounter on your journey. I thought about the Children of Israel, while they traveled through the wilderness. Deuteronomy 8:4 says: Thy raiment waxed not old upon thee, neither did thy foot swell, these forty years, he preserved their clothing throughout the journey. They weren't perfect people and had to be constantly reminded of what the Lord had already done. The Lord continued to feed, guide and protect them all the way. It took them longer than it was supposed to because they complained and got distracted but when they got focused they finally made it. So, this garment is not tailor made but Word made. The bible says in Ephesians 6:10, 11: Finally, my brethren, be strong in the Lord, and in the power of his might. Put on the whole armor of God that ye may be able to stand against the wiles of the devil. Only God's armor can protect you in every battle of your life. Continue trusting him, believing him, and never doubting him. Only the Lord can give you strength and power to stand against the snare of the fowler. The Lord is the same yesterday, today and even forever more.

I began to ponder many questions in my mind. What do I need to do and how long do I need to be in his presence? Many years of tears, heartaches and pain, I continued pressing, fasting, praying and believing in the Lord. Many years of rejection, and being not important to others, God was yet working on the garment. All through school, talked about, criticize, judged and laughed at. Many times, I would give in. I wanted to be like others, but soon realized what if I lost my life and went to hell, so I would find myself. I would find myself repenting over-and-over again, because I wanted to be pleasing in the Lord's eyes. I realized the greater the blessings the greater the trial. So, in the making of the garment, there were opinions of others jokes, lies, backbiting, backstabbing and the attacks against me but the word sustained me. Romans 8:18 says that: I reckon that the sufferings of this present time are not worthy to be compared with the glory which shall be revealed in us. I also had to realize, even though the devil was always on my trail, trying to hinder the journey and assignment in my life, the Lord loved me. The devil was trying to

> I realize the greater the blessings the greater the trial.

confuse me about who I was, but the love of the Saints, their prayers, and encouragement, helped to keep my mind stayed on him. There are lyrics to a song that says; EVERYWHERE YOU GO THERE IS TROUBLE, EVERYWHERE YOU GO, THERE IS STRIFE, and EVERYWHERE YOU GO THERE IS SOMETHING THAT WORRIES YOU BUT REMEMBER THAT OUR GOD IS STANDING BY. It got really difficult sometimes, many tears shed because of rejection but Lord was right there with me and I had to realize that I couldn't travel with confidence, trust in the Lord and listening to what others thought about me at the same time. Therefore, this garment of worship couldn't have pockets nor should I say baggage.

Sometimes we carry unnecessary baggage. We hold on to things, situations, circumstances that hinder us from receiving miracles, healings, and blessings. The bible says in Hebrews 12:1: "Wherefore seeing we also are compassed about with so great a cloud of witnesses, let us lay aside every weight, and the sin which doth so easily beset us, and let us run with patience the race that is set before us"; But there's a difference between the natural and spiritual garments. In natural garments, the seamstress can sew and make alterations to fit the outside of our body. You can even go to the store and buy garments for whatever the occasion may be in different colors, sizes, and shapes. But in spiritual garments, only the Lord can create you for his purpose. Your body is the temple of the Holy Ghost. "Know ye not that your bodies are the members of Christ" (1st Corinthians 6:15). When we live for the Lord, he guides us. We have to know his purpose in us. Allow God to build you and not man then you will know what you are called to do.

The Spirit of the Lord God is upon me; because the Lord hath anointed me to preach good tidings unto the meek; he hath sent me to bind up the brokenhearted, to proclaim liberty to the captives, and the opening of the prison to them that are bound; To proclaim the acceptable year of the Lord, and the day of vengeance of our God; to comfort all that mourn; To appoint unto them that mourn in Zion, to give unto them beauty for ashes, the oil of joy for mourning, the GARMENT OF PRAISE for the spirit of heaviness; that they might be called trees of righteousness, the planting of the Lord, that he might be glorified. (Isaiah 61:1-2)

On the outside, I may look like I just got off the clearance rack or come from a garage sale, but there was much value on the inside.

We are God's design, his creation, knowing the joy, the peace, and love that he gives; the world can't take it away. The spiritual garment is created in the mind of God and he uses us that he might be glorified. He didn't have to purchase the pattern; it wasn't predesigned or manufactured, neither from any other god nor in the mind of man. It wasn't shipped by car, boat, airplane, train and the yards weren't premeasured by a tailor. His plans weren't given to any man to create or design. The garment didn't look good in its first stages. I had to realize as a young girl that I may not have felt like I was qualified or capable of doing what the Lord wanted me to do. I was talked about because of what I look like on the outside. People labeled me by what I wore on the outside but on the inside, they couldn't see that the anointing of the Lord was stirring in my belly. They couldn't see how much I loved the Lord and how determined I was, to hold on and make this journey. They were quick to judge my outer appearance and couldn't see that God was making a vessel fit for his use. It reminds me of a beautiful flower, we only focus on what we see, the color, the beauty of it, and rarely do we think about what it had to go through in the dirt. We look at the glory and don't know the story. While experiencing different obstacles of life, he was building the foundation that was needed to withstand the storms and hindrances ahead. So, man looked at me as rumble, incapable, a liability, and didn't look in me and see the work in progress. God had his hands on me and the more I learn of him, the more he released that word in the garment (temple). I had to keep moving forward despite of rejection. Some were waiting to see me give up and fall flat on my face. People even said I would never be a fit vessel. Many days I felt broken, torn, misuse and out of place. I felt as though, I could not take another step, but in the midst of it all I felt the love of God holding me and

> We look at the glory and don't know the story.

comforting me. I love the lyrics to the song that says: REACH BEYOND THE BREAK AND HOLD ON. Thank God for one set of foot prints. LORD YOU CARRIED ME!

We experience and will experience many storms in our lifetime. Some will make us and others will try to break us. Dr. M. DeWayne Anderson wrote a statement: The Holy Spirit is provoking changes in your life. He went on to say that the Lord is not satisfied with us being stagnant, static or immature. The Holy Spirit comforts us and makes intercession for us. When we receive the word of the Lord in our hearts it begins the process of transforming us in the image and likeness of the Lord Jesus Christ. I prayed to the Lord many times concerning this book and he spoke it clearly to me. GARMENT OF

WORSHIP. Repeatedly; I kept saying garment of worship, garment of worship. I begin to ask, what is that all about? I asked myself GARMENT OF WORSHIP what? I didn't understand at first, but the Lord began to reveal more to me in the word; I Corinthians 6:17 say: But he that is joined unto the lord is one spirit. Then the Word read in 1 Corinthians 6:19—What? Know ye not that your body is the temple of the Holy Ghost, which is in you, which ye have of God, and ye are not your own? Wow, I belong to God and not man. The garment that God created was in his mind in the beginning and it was birthed naturally with my mom and dad and manifested when I heard the word, received the word, believed the word and gave God my life. I was shifted; pulled on, pushed aside, but God kept doing the work in me. In the midst of lies, abuse, mistreatment, God kept his hands on me and did not change the assignment. I had a big appetite for the knowledge of God's word. I began to latch on to the word and was desperate for his will. Just like in the natural you get thirsty and hungry for food and water which helps to nourish you so you can grow and be healthy. Matthew 5:6 'Blessed are they which do hunger and thirst after righteousness, for they shall be filled'. I didn't fully understand entirely what the Lord was doing in me, but the craving to learn more and more about him grew more and more in my heart. The more experiences there were became a birthing of another level of learning. Even though, I was excited about the Lord and very faithful in the services and etc. Many times I would cry because I thought my dedication to the church, fasting, prayers, my faithfulness, singing in the choir, teaching Sunday School, that God would go ahead and give me what I wanted, needed, and bless me abundantly. Right then every time I thought the blessings would be nonstop daily and flow continuously. I shouted and danced, I witnessed, I cleaned the church, and I took the word of great value in Psalms 46:1—God is our refuge and strength, a very PRESENT HELP IN TROUBLE. When it said present, I thought it meant soon as you ask but it also meant peace, joy, and strength in the midst of your storm. Really, I was trying to make God and not letting God make me.

The Lord spoke and said to me: Le me do it Leslie at my time, but if I do it all at one time the garment wouldn't be durable, it wouldn't be complete and it wouldn't be able to hold out in the different seasons that are coming your way. This garment had to be durable enough to witness to others that were not saved, that were broken, and wounded. He said, if you don't let me lead you it would not be a garment of Worship, but you would be a showcase for the theater. Jeremiah 29:11 says that for I know the thoughts that I think toward you, saith the Lord, thoughts of peace and not of evil, to give you an expected end. So, the Lord was making me and preparing me for the journey. He didn't want to build me with material things, but with the anointing. Ephesians 2:10—for we are his workmanship, created in Christ Jesus unto good works, which God hath before ordained that we should walk in them.

So, the more I let go and let God, the more came wisdom and, the knowledge. I begin more and more giving him the praise and glory for what he was unfolding and revealing in little ole dusty me. The word was sustaining me, giving me the determination and the ability to run on and endure hardness as a good soldier. Even when the enemy came, the Lord was with me and giving me the strength I needed to go through. My love became stronger and my heart loved him more.

Chapter 3

GARMENT FIT FOR THE MASTER'S USE

If a man therefore purge himself from these, he shall be a vessel unto honor, sanctified, and meet for the master's use, and prepared unto every good work (2nd Timothy 2:21)

In this world, there are a lot of things that we face and a lot of uncertainties and dilemmas that we encounter that we didn't sign up for. Some things are pleasant and others are not pleasant at all. We need assurance of who we are and whose we are? It's like taking a natural flight. We need a Pilot that not only to fly but get us to our destination safely. In spite of all I went through in school, I could not have made it without him being my Pilot, instructor, deliverer, and guidance counselor. Those days in school can hold a chapter by themselves. In school was where I really said yes Lord.

Giving my life to the Lord in High School had some major challenges. I was a basketball player and back in the day, the saints didn't believe in wearing pants. I really wanted to be saved but I was allowing what people were saying get next to me. When I graduated from high school, I did not go and play basketball in college because I thought I could not be saved, playing basketball and wearing shorts. There were some extreme situations that were going on in my personal life that was really taking a toll on me both mentally and physically. Some people tried to figure out what I could possibly be going through being so young, but the devil didn't care about my age, or anything else. He was plotting to destroy my mind and my determination to get more acquainted with God. Satan, love doing his job, he never takes vacation or days off. He goes to and fro, seeking whom he may devour. Daily, he pulls at you, tries to hinder you, and distract you from doing what the Lord told you to do. He will do anything to make you fill like you are not fit to do kingdom work. He will even use others to say or do things to try to discourage you or make you feel unworthy to do the Lord's work. Every time the devil reminds you of your past, remind him of his future. He is like a thief. John 10:10—the thief cometh not, but for to steal, and to kill, and to destroy; I am come that they might have life, and that they might have it more abundantly. We must know without a doubt that your relationship with the Lord stands assure. I went through a lot of situations in my teenage years. The only thing I had to hold on to was God's Love, Grace and Mercy.

Many days I felt no love. I felt that nobody cared. Even in a crowd it felt like loneliness was my best friend. I felt like giving up. I did everything I could to stay around the Saints, the prayers, the services, they were my comfort and security blanket. I really needed to know that the Lord cared about me. Whatever the challenges, tests, trials, tribulations in my life; the Lord knew what to do, how to do and when to do it. He kept me in my right mind and comforted me daily. I heard many Saints testify that the Lord was the head of their lives and pray their strength in the Lord. It didn't' matter whether they had a home, car, food, money or not, they would praise and worship the Lord continuously. I know that life was not perfect for them, but they appreciated what they had and continued to believe that the Lord would provide. I wanted that same determination they had. I really wanted God to use me. That desire to live for him became serious and I began to fast and pray for the answer I was searching for. When I was very young I repeatedly heard the Saints tell me that I was a Missionary and God is going to use me. Those words sounded so precious and exciting, but I wanted to know it for myself. So, fasting, praying, and shut-ins were a priority in my life. I took interest in learning and studying about being chosen. I often asked myself, was I good enough to witness to others about the Lord. I wanted to be saved and I wanted to know did the Lord forgive me of all my sins. I didn't want my soul to be lost. I wanted to be confident that this was the Lord's plan for my life and not my own thinking and decision. God didn't choose me because of my clothes, money, or talent, he chose me because he knew me from the beginning, the plans for my life. Even when I felt useless, unfit, lonely, hungry, thirsty, down, discouraged, the Lord was still there. He comforted me when my days were treacherous, and I dreamed the worst nightmares that were happening while I was sleeping. The Lord was there every time the enemy came to consume me. When I knew that God wanted to use my life as a vessel chosen, there were steps of growth, and things I had to go through. Every day wasn't peaches and cream, neither was the sun shining, but the Lord continued to put his word down on the inside. I had to know that even though some days seem cloudy, there was a brighter day coming. Even though the battle wasn't over, I was learning that I could walk in victory. I was reminded that if he did it before he can do it again. God used ordinary people to carry his work and be a witness for him. Even though we are saved, chosen, called, or sent, we will have to suffer and go through some things. 2 Timothy 2:12a says: If we suffer, we shall also reign with him. I realize that we can't choose what to suffer, never choose how long to suffer when we suffer, because if God let us choose, it wouldn't be growth, it would be pleasure. So, God wants the glory out

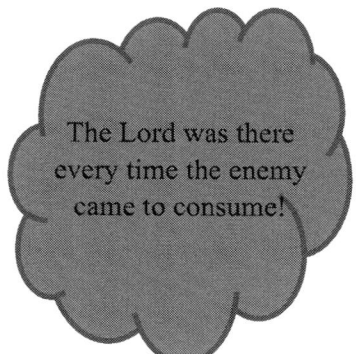

> The Lord was there every time the enemy came to consume!

of our lives. He is not going to share his glory with anybody. But his word is his bond, and whatever his word says, it SHALL COME TO PASS.... yes Lord!!!!

I kept praying that the Lord would continue to teach me about being chosen. I often wondered, asking myself, am I really chosen, and can I really be a vessel fit for the master's use? Although, I was learning about being chosen, I also knew that Satan didn't want me to do kingdom work. I was finding out more and more that the enemy will never be my friend. The bible says in Job 1:6, Now there was a day when the sons of God came to present themselves before the LORD, and Satan came also among them. Satan didn't have any respect for my situation, he was attacking me. I had to keep praying and giving praises to the Lord. The more I said YES LORD, the more the enemy tried to make me feel like God didn't love me and I didn't meet the requirements to be a kingdom representative. When I went to church the devil didn't stay outside, he came to the church and in the church, trying to hinder people from being blessed. There were days I felt down but God's love lifted me. I also had to learn to pray and fast more at home too. Whatever I was experiencing, he gave me comfort, strength and peace to hold on and hold out. OH…the Lord was manifesting his word in my heart and it was evident that the foundation was firm and strong. I started not only testifying about how he saved me but I started being a witness of his miracles and blessings. I am chosen and I am a vessel fit for the master's use. He was working on me and I was

excited to know that he chose me to be a part of the kingdom assignment. I couldn't see him nor could I see his hands, but I felt him and this great potter was doing a great work with some messed up clay. I realized he was a perfect seamstress and he was creating and a making me. I was a GARMENT IN THE MAKING. When I felt unskilled, uneducated, the Lord was still working on mind, my heart. I kept reading and learning more about the word. He kept sewing and stitching the broken me, the torn me, the discourage me. When it seems as though no one walking on the earth had the answer or solution, the Lord made me storm proof and designed me to weather any climate and withstand anything I was going to face. Many times, I didn't know how or what to pray, the word says
in Romans 8:26 says: Likewise the Spirit also

helpeth our infirmities: for we know not what we should pray for as we ought: but the Spirit itself maketh intercession for us with groanings which cannot be uttered.

Many years were going by and many times I struggled to hold on to God. I kept repenting, asking the Lord to forgive me for not following his instructions. Even when I felt no one was there to encourage me, I had to encourage myself in the Lord. Be careful with your walk with the Lord. If you are not focused the devil will take advantage of it. He is waiting for us to doubt the word and we need the word to complete the task. It's like I needed a cap to the bottle or can I say, icing on the cake. I needed the Holy Ghost. The bible says: John 14:16: And I pray the Father, and he shall give you another comforter, that he may abide with you forever. God will comfort you and protect you and give you his whole armor so that you are strong enough to stand and come out victoriously. The bible says in John 14:26-but the Comforter, which is the Holy Ghost, whom the Father will send in my name, he shall teach you all things, and bring all things to your remembrance, whatsoever I have said unto you. Oh, the Lord had me all covered all the way around, a full circle. Yes I'm chosen, covered and shielded. Psalm 20:7: Some trust in chariots, and some in horses: but we will remember the name of the Lord our God. I may not know all about him, but the little I know, I truly trust him. Although my family didn't understand what the Lord was doing in me. My mom knew she was carrying a baby but did not know that God had chosen her baby girl.

From the beginning, the call of the Lord was invisible, but down on the inside it was growing and maturing year after year. Even when I didn't know the Lord had already begun the normal in my life. The more I let God be God, the more he continued to work on me. My mom didn't know that she was carrying a garment of worship; she didn't know she was carrying a child that was going to be use by the Lord. But Lord, I thank you for choosing this rag to work with. Things that went on in my life, toss me to here and there. Many nights I cried, restless and uncomfortable. The devil tried to convince me that God didn't care. The devil took the tragedies and challenges in my life and used them against me. He tried to make me feel there's no way I can walk victorious, be a winner, or be a witness for the Lord. While riding through the storm, prayer and fasting kept me more focused on God's plan than on the devil's plot. Isaiah 26: 3 says: "Thou will keep him in perfect peace, whose mind is stayed on thee because he trusteth in thee". God knows the ending before the beginning begins. It's up to us whether we grasp the word to journey the assignment or choose to do it on our own, which is not a good choice. So, when the Lord sends you out, believe me, he has already equipped you with everything you need. We can do it with the Lord's help and his power. We can run through troops and leap over walls with the Lord on our side. We can win the battles with the Lord on our side. The word says that he who began a good work in you must complete it. Although, we don't understand the complete journey, the Lord knows all things, trust him to lead you. Even when weapons form, God is our shield and protection. Knowing that things are going to come against you, some people are not going to accept the new normal in your life. Isaiah 54:17 says: No weapon that is formed against thee shall prosper and every tongue that rises up against thee in judgment thou shalt condemn. Don't fear, don't give up, God will take care of you and bring you through it all. REMEMBER IF YOU WORK THE WORD THE WORD WILL WORK FOR YOU. GLORY!!! Philippians 4:7 says : And the Peace of God that surpasses all understanding shall keep your hearts and mind through Christ Jesus. You are not exempted, from the devil's attacks. We will have challenges, obstacles and tribulations. 1st Peter 1:7-9 say--These trials are only to test your faith, to see whether or not it is strong and pure. It is being tested as fire tests gold and purifies it-and your faith is far more precious to God than mere gold; if your faith remains strong after being tried in the test tube of fiery trials, it will bring you much praise and glory and honor on the day of his return. Tests come not just to make you strong but to see how strong your faith is. I was learning more and more to trust a God that I could not see. No one desires or ask for trouble, storms, test, trials, or tribulations. Learning that things were going to happen regardless of who I was or where I came from. Every mountain may not move, you may have to climb some of them. Are you equipped for the climb? Are you prepared for the obstacle course? The travel is not easy all the time. You got to be confident that the Lord is always there and he is everywhere at the same time.

The saints always prayed and encouraged me. They told me to hold on. God is going to use you one day, they said. I thought all the Saints were sweet, but every now and then some would be negative. Sometimes you will get hurt in church, but don't give up on God because he won't give up on you. I remembered crying one day at church because of negative words I heard a lady say. A mother of the church walks up to me, instead of comforting my hurt, and wiping my tears, said; Sister Leslie, you better get a backbone. She was letting me know, even though you are chosen, saved, sanctified and love the Lord. You are going to be under attack, not just from the worldly people but those that are in church too. I had to realize that the world is not the only ones that will come against you. Sometimes you get church hurt. The Saints kept telling me to hold on; God will answer your prayers. Those words sounded good to my ears, but I didn't know everything I had to go through. I like the sound of God using me. I didn't know that suffering help to give birth to the good character and the anointing. Bishop Patterson always said SALVATION IS FREE, BUT IT COST. You get more strength going through than your blessings being put in your hand. I have been through some harsh, embarrassing, overwhelming, cruel and mental abuse in life, but it was all in the making of me. I'm not walking this journey by myself, the Lord is here with me every step and it's been worth it. Even when I felt alone, he was there. I had to keep praying and be confident that he was there all the time. I thank God that he was there every time the snare of the enemy tried to consume me. I thank

God for every deposit of his word and realize there is a word for every trial, test, tribulation that tries to distract the journey in my life. There were times when I felt like given up because I didn't have a friend that could really see what was really going inside of me. The more I was learning about holiness, the more I was feeling the Lord's presence in my life. Even though I could not see him his presence was so profound. I could feel his love. As years were passing the more the assignment was relevant to me.

The movement of God changed the entire identity of my life. I started noticing that whenever trials and test come, the more he was bringing me through, teaching and showing me the way to victory. Every time the devil plotted, God was ahead of him with the plan and the way of escape. Every time the waves and tides got high in my life, the Lord was there speaking to the winds saying PEACE BE STILL… Even though, I didn't have all that I wanted in life; his peace meant more to me. Many people get excited about material things in life, meaning some people are out of control and think material things are all that. I'm not knocking any of that, because I like nice things to, but a relationship with the Lord is so important than anything. But we are going to go through some things, even gold had to go through the fire to become a beautiful and valuable item. Everything invented go through a process to become what it is. Some things have to die, be sacrifice, or leave its original state or place. We were lost but Jesus died for our sins that we might live, that we may have life and life more abundantly. Oh, my Lord, now that is love. John 15:13: Greater love hath no man than this, that a man lay down his life for friends. Thank God for the call, the plans for my life. Thank God that he loves us and wants to bless us. Being chosen is not a result of our bank accounts, our family heritage, who we knew, or what community we live in. He didn't hold it against us when Adam mess up. He didn't change the promise when I mess up. He still loved me and helps me daily. I knew that God wanted to use my life as a garment of worship. There were so many things I had to learn even at the beginning of the journey in doing the will of the Lord. I had to have a backbone. I had to continue to read and study the word of God. I had to learn and yet learning to hear the Lord's voice. I don't always get it all right, sometimes we fall short, but the Lord has compassion. The bible says that Lamentations 3:22,23—It is of the Lord's mercies that we are not consumed, because his compassions fail not. They are new every morning: great is thy faithfulness. I had to be confident and know the Lord was my guide and he was right there by my side. Many saints have traveled and traveling this journey of Holiness and I always observe the Saints dedication and their commitment to God. They stayed on their knees and believed that the Lord could do the impossible. I was so encouraged to see that even though they suffered, was persecuted, lied on, talked about, didn't have much, they kept trusting and praising the lord. I learned a lot and desperately wanted to obtain what I needed to survive daily. If it had not been for the Lord on my side, life would be worthless, like an airplane without a pilot. It was evident that the hand of the Lord was on my life and he was molding me to be a vessel fit for the master's use. Obtaining a prayer life, consistent in seeking him was easier said than done. I have confident in the Lord and I know that he will never ever leave me COMFORTLESS.

Chapter 4

Reachable

**I am crucified with Christ: nevertheless I live; yet not I, but Christ liveth in me: and the life which I now live in the flesh I live by the faith of the Son of god, who loved me, and gave himself for me.
(Galatians 5:20)**

Years are passing and I'm yet eager to learn more and more about the Lord in my life. Some things are still up for questioning, although I have to learn to be content. I'm learning not to be just chosen but reachable. In that you have to be patient and wait on God's time and work in the place and stated you are in. Ephesians 3:4 says: Whereby when ye read, ye may understand my knowledge and the mystery of Christ. Continue speaking life, his word and his will to your existence. Reachable is another level in life with Christ. My desire to be totally committed and sold out for the Lord was growing. There are so many things in life to do. There are so many things that we obligate ourselves to. What is priority? What is most important? We will never be able to completely figure out God's design and his plan. He knows what he has design, the total you and what your purpose is. To know your purpose but to be reachable is another. What does reachable mean? How much of me really available to the Lord. I know I can't serve two masters. I'm I really going in the right direction and doing what he has call for me to do. I know that the Lord is my strong tower, my everlasting peace. You can't do satan and the Lord at the same time, you have to trust in the Lord all the way.

Proverbs 3:5-6 says Trust in the Lord with all thine heart: and lean not unto thine own understanding. In all thy ways acknowledge him, and he shall direct thy paths. These scriptures have been a part of my life for a long time, learning how to trust and obey a God that I can't see. I often think about how and why he really created us. But if the Lord made the day and knew what to put in the day. Even before I was thought of, he knew me and the purpose for my existence. Again the word of the Lord says in Jeremiah 29:11---I know the thoughts that I toward you to prosper you and give you an expected end. You see, it's a blessing to know he has already thought what we are thinking or what we are in question about. We will never be able to completely figure out the way God puts things together. With all the tug of war challenges of life, the Lord knows what to do and how to do it. You cannot give half of your days to the devil and the other half to God and desire the anointing. Even though trials come on every hand, you have still have to keep your eyes and focus on him. He will give you power to endure. Continue to pray boldly until you know you have the Lord's attention. I don't care how broken, how torn, how difficult it may seem, the Lord can resolve it, solve it, mend it, lift it, and strengthen it. Joshua 1:9 says: Yea be bold and strong: banish fear and doubt for remember the Lord your God is with you wherever you go. Remember be reachable and available. You really must stay focus and trust God. It's not all the time you will feel like it. Your flesh may not be in the mood to push, but you got to keep praying and believing. Matthew 26:41: Watch and pray, that you enter not into temptation: the spirit indeed is willing, but the flesh is weak. You don't have to go far to meet opposition. It is right there with you. Although you must strive to do his will to be honest, it is easier said than done. But you can't do it without faith. Saying is one thing and doing is another. But they work together. James 2:17-Even so faith, if it has not works, is dead, being alone. No matter how dedicated, reachable, committed you are, there are still things you will face in life. YOU ARE NOT EXEMPTED.

Song says: My hope is built on nothing less than Jesus blood and righteousness. So, when I started hearing and receiving the message for my life. The foundation of holiness was really beginning to manifest in my heart and mind. I then began a YES LORD in my heart. I could fill the Lord changing my DNA spiritually. I reflect in my life about how far God has brought me. Sometimes I even think about the day I made up in my mind that this is truly the way to be, to be in the will of the Lord. Oh, seeking the Lord was my heart's desire. I wanted to be a genuine, true worshiper. I wanted the Lord in my life so much and I wanted to be confident that he was directing my path. What conversation the natural garment would have if it could talk every time it was cut, sewed, pulled, washed, dried. WOW!! What if the clay could talk every time the potter had to remold it, spin it and heat it? If the wood could holler every time it sees the sight of a nail, hammer or saw. But what comfort we have that in times whether good or bad, help is on the way. The garment of worship has a comforter, a provider, a sustainer, a mender and an everlasting helper. I Corinthian 4:16---Know ye not that ye are the temple of God and that the Spirit of God dwelleth in you. There's a sweet relief in knowing that the Lord is always there and always in reach while you are on the journey. You must know who you are and whose you are. Seeking the Lord for revelation of the word takes faith and focus. I had to realize that God didn't tell everybody to do the same thing and it's easy to get distracted. He didn't tell everybody what my assignment was or is. In that, everybody is not going to understand. Sometimes you have more opposition in doing God's will than close friends. I tell people that how can a bird that never left the nest, teach you how to fly? Sometimes people have poor judgment about others, but you don't have to listen to it or follow them. You would think that everyone is happy about your relationship with God. I remember days when I felt as if I was in quick sand. There were people standing on dry land with life jackets and would not help me. I was mad and soon realized they couldn't help me because they could not help themselves. You will have some people that will never accept what you are doing. Some will even say, it's not the thing to do. Don't slack, be reachable. Whenever the Lord has to pour in you, be available.

I realize that the enemy will make you feel unreachable because of what you have done in the past, or what has happened to you in the past. I had to be careful sharing what the Lord had given me. Everybody is not going to believe you or receive you. Ephesians 4:17-24 says: This I say therefore, and testify in the Lord, that ye henceforth walk not as other Gentiles walk, in the vanity of their mind, Having the understanding darkened, being alienated from the life of God through the ignorance that is in them, because of the blindness of their heart: Who being past feeling have given themselves over unto lasciviousness, to work all uncleanness with greediness. But ye have not so learned Christ; If so be that ye have heard him, and have been taught by him, as the truth is in Jesus: That ye put off concerning the former conversation the old man, which is corrupt according to the deceitful lusts; and be renewed in the spirit of your mind; And that ye put on the new man, which after God is created in righteousness and true holiness. Even though sometimes I feel discouraged, I always find my way to an atmosphere of encouragement and strength. It's so comforting to pray and seek the Lord anytime you desire. Psalm 16:11-Thou will show me the path of life: in thy presence is fullness of joy; at thy right hand there are pleasures for evermore. So why keep listening to those that couldn't see the assignment of the Lord in me especially if they aren't believers themselves. I had to realize that the Lord didn't tell everybody what he wanted me to do, neither did he tell me to tell everybody. Some thought I was too young, wasn't ready and others thought no not you. I was young yet learning his voice and when he speaks to me. I wanted to know that it wasn't just me talking but it was truly the Lord telling what to do. All I needed was his validation and his approval.

Whether people believe in me or not, all I have to do is keep moving forward in his direction. Everybody's not spiritual minded. They may be intelligent, older and have good advice, but it still may not be the right advice. Romans 8:6-for to be carnally minded is death: but to be spiritually minded is life and peace. Carnal minds can't define spiritual things. We walk by faith and not by sight. You must stay focus and have faith. Being reachable, helps you to be accessible and available to do your assignment and be pleasing to the Lord. So, faith cometh by hearing and hearing by the word of God. The more of the word I heard, the more attentive I was to the voice of the Lord. No matter what I had done or mistakes I had made, I was reachable and I could still feel the Lord helping me and strengthening me daily. Sometimes it's lonely during the making of you. Desiring the real love of the Lord in your life sometimes calls for desperate measures, but you can make it and surely you can take it. Have confidence in God's armor. Study the word of the Lord and be of good courage. The battle is not yours; it belongs to the Lord. Let God lead and guide you all the way. On this journey there may be some road blocks and detours but God's word is our compass. Just go forth with no restraint, God has you.

While the Lord was creating the garment, he guarded it, protected it that it could with stand against any attacks of the enemy. It could withstand during any storms that I had to weather. I realize just being saved wasn't all of it. I knew there was a work that the Lord wanted me to do. To be a witness and a steward of his word was what he wanted. Some days when I needed clarity, when I prayed, it felt like he was not listening, he had left me. In those times he was stretching my reach. He was building me. You never know how out of shape you are until you start stretching. When the storms of life were raging, I prayed to be rescued out of it, yet he allowed me to go through it to better my relationship and trust in him. I had to realize that the message of the storm was beyond my expectations. He didn't let me die, be consumed, or be defeated. Even when I had other attacks of life, he was there all the time to strengthen me. When friends change like seasons, the Lord stayed the same. I could go to the rock of my salvation and I can always lean on him. Psalms 27:1—The Lord is my light and my salvation; whom shall I fear? The Lord is the strength of my life; of whom shall I be afraid? In knowing that he was my protector, my comfort, my all and all, I could sense the flavor for my Savior. I thank God for the assignment in my life. Even though the journey is not always easy, the Lord had a way to bring me through, over, and out victoriously. I was learning how to be reachable to him, who was always reachable to me. One of the extraordinary things about the Lord was that he chose little me, from a small town. I had no predecessors in my family. But he chose me and I'm so GRATEFUL. Even when I was a little girl and didn't know this new normal, the Lord still love me. Even though the enemy was trying to attack my life constantly, the saints kept praying for me and encouraging me to keep my eyes on the Lord and be humble.   I wanted my relationship with the Lord so good, that whenever he needed somebody, I was not only available, but I was REACHABLE.

I pray that this book you are reading is benefits not only to you, but your families, neighbors, coworkers. I pray that you not just read it but that it will help your walk with the Lord. A car is not useful if it doesn't have a driver. You can't reach your destination if you don't know where you are going. You will never get anywhere if you keep letting stuff stand in your way. So, I wanted to encourage others that maybe stuck and feel like they are not qualified for kingdom work. I wanted to be able to do what the Lord wanted me to do anytime and anywhere. That means that his word had to dwell in me and not just be a visiting. Have we become so busy with life that the Lord is not priority in our life?

All of us have a purpose, but are we REACHABLE, or available for the Lord.

Chapter 5

Spiritual Maintenance

Being confident of this very thing, that he which hath begun a good work in you will perform it until the day of Jesus Christ.
Philippians 1:6

As I travel this journey as God's chosen vessel, I had to learn that God had not only started a beginning in my life that I was unaware of, but the call was already equipped. Although the storms, trials, test, tribulation that I experienced sometimes caused me to tremble, wavier, or be a little fearful, the Lord already was a step ahead with victory results. Let me go further to say that maintenance on my life required the hand of God to continue molding my life daily. He had to deliver the me out of me. We all need spiritual maintenance in our lives to help sustain us and keep us safe against life's challenges. Just like cars, furnaces, AC units, just to name a few, need maintenance, so do we need it. We need the Lord, not a quick fix, a soothsayer, a palm reader, or idol. We need God daily to work on us. We need to continue studying the word of the Lord that it may instruct us on what to do, how to do, and when to do. The more I allowed him to work on my mind the more I knew that he was with me all the way, through thick and then. A man can do only so much for us, take us so far and what a man gives is so limited. Ephesians

3:20: Now to unto him that is able to do exceeding abundantly above all that we ask or think, according to the power that worketh in us. Nevertheless, we don't ever have to worry. If he brings us to it then he has equipped us already to go through it. Someone once said if you can stand the pull he'll pull you through. When I felt like given up, the maintenance of the word was saying hold on. When I felt like I couldn't make another step, the maintenance of the word said, I'm the light unto your path and a lamp unto your feet. I realize then that everything that I needed was in the word of God. I realize the more I depended on him the more he shielded me, embraced me and covered me all the way. The weathers of life try to affect your focus and relationship with the Lord. Distraction, detours, hindrances wanted me to feel useless, worthless to the kingdom. But the maintenance word of God mends the brokenness, the word of God heals the hurt, the word of God calms the storm, and the word of God delivers me out of captivity. Psalm 34:19-Many are the afflictions of the righteous: but the Lord delivereth him out of them all. What I'm saying is there's a word for the BROKEN YOU, THE TORN YOU, THE SICK YOU, THE DIVORCE YOU, THE UPSIDE DOWN YOU, THE BACKSLIDING YOU, THE WEAK YOU, and THE OPPRESS YOU.

The word of Oswald Chambers says: LEAVE THE BROKEN, IRREVERSIBLE PAST IN GOD'S HANDS, AND STEP OUT INTO THE INVINCIBLE FUTURE WITH HIM, while experiencing an impartation of his word, the more I was trying to let the Lord be Lord over my life, he also had to break down me and I had to die and crucify the flesh daily. You have to know in your walk that there is enough in God to take you all the way. I needed an attitude adjustment. I needed a personality alignment. My attitude needed an oil change and my heart needed a tune up. Someone said your attitude determines your altitude. The Lord had to give maintenance on the inside of me. I needed more than a testimony that the Lord save me. I need a continuance of his presence, after he pick me up, after he forgave me of my sins, after he place my feet on a solid rock to stay. I needed the Holy Ghost, the comforter, the peace of God in my heart. When no one else could help me, I knew the comforter was there to keep me. The more I obeyed the Lord the more the enemy attacked me. The More I said yes Lord, the more the enemy said:

I'm coming. This garment, regardless of the situation and circumstances that come up in my life. He kept strengthen me, endowing me with the power of the Holy Ghost. I kept praising, magnifying him giving him all the glory. I kept fast and praying that he would continue working on me. Lied on, he kept working on me, abused, he kept working on me, church hurt, he kept working on me, sick, he kept working on me. I needed maintenance all the time. Dark days, I kept praising him, broke days I kept praising him. Spiritual maintenance renews your strength with joy, peace and understanding. Sometimes our desires in life detours us from the will of the Lord. James 1:15—then when lust hath conceived, it bringeth forth sin: and sin, when it is finished, bringeth forth death. When Eve in Genesis 3:6 saw the fruit on the tree, it looked good to see and eat, but it wasn't good for them. What looks good may not be right for you. The Lord is the potter (maintenance Man) and I am the clay…..He can put you back together again...Even when situations in my life was devastating and almost carved me into a brick model, the Lord continued to pour into me his word and he embraced me in my lonest hours.

I learn to really get the Lord's attention through prayer. Many days I prayed to the Lord to pour on me, touch me Lord, make me over again, and bind the devil, save me Lord. Praying to the Lord to help develop the relationship with him was more important than the material things of life. Many days the garment was attacked and challenged by the enemy, but the Lord was strengthening me and giving me much needed peace. I prayed for tools in his word to fix me, heal me, develop me so I can be a witness, and a good steward of his word. A good swimmer is not intimidated by large bodies of water. Howbeit, those that cannot swim are intimidated by ponds. But knowing that the Lord is by your side always, assures you that no mountain is too high, no valley too low, NO RIVER TOO WIDE, that he can't bring you through. I was confident that whatever the garment needed, or whatever it had to weather or encounter, the hand and plan of God was well prepared for it. The Lord can use what he wants, how he wants and when he wants to use it. God can take the ordinary and do extraordinary things with it. God can speak to the wind, water, fire, lions, storms, and the rain. He is an on time, in time God and all the time God. It is good to know that he has you on his mind.

Sometimes we encounter things in our life that may cause us to worry, if we allow God to take care of the minor problems then the major problem can't come forth. The devil comes to try and hinder, stop and distracts us. He wants us to give up when things are tough and rough. He wants us to feel like that we are not capable of being use by the Lord.

> This is a faithful saying, and these things I will that thou affirm constantly, that they which have believed in God might be careful to maintain good works. These things are good and profitable unto men.
> (Titus 3:8)

We cannot forget where we come from and how far God has brought us. In this, allow him to work on us daily. Seek him consistently, study his word and complete the work.

Chapter 6

Benefits of Obedience

Blessed be the Lord, who daily loadeth us with benefits, even the god of our Salvation. Selah.
(Psalm 68:19)

Obedience is better than a sacrifice. The dictionary says that obedience, human behavior, is a form of social influence in which a person yields to explicit instructions or orders from an authority figure. Obedience comes when you really love and commit to the word of God. Not just reading but being a doer of his word. There are great benefits in the natural life when you are following the rules, obeying your parents and following the rules of the home. There must be some order. First, in order to reap the benefits, you got to sow sparingly. Second, you got to stay focus. We are not exempted from trouble. You will have some detours, tests, road blocks and some obstacles, but keep your eyes on the prize. The blessings on your life, the promises released to you, your family, your children and your companion. Philippians 3:14-'I press toward the mark for the prize of the high calling of God in Christ Jesus'. Be confident that no matter what you experience in life, if you stay on the Lord's side, you will receive what he has promised you. We have a choice whether to do right or to do wrong. We have a choice whether to conform to this world or be transformed by the renewing of our minds. If we obey him then there is no limit what will do for us. If we obey him, there is so much wealth for our lives. The Lord has so many blessings for our lives, but it comes with being obedient. If we are in the will of the Lord, there is nothing that he will withhold from us. Isaiah 1:19-20 says; If ye be willing and obedient, ye shall eat the good of the land: A lot of people miss blessings and promises in the bible because of disobedience, trying to do it their way. Moses missed Canaan, Lot's wife looked back, Adam and Eve were disobedient, Jonah was disobedient and many more. Obedience pays off. But if ye refuse and rebel, ye shall be devoured with the sword: for the mouth of the Lord hath spoken it. We must know that the Lord already has a plan for our lives, but it is under condition. You have to love the Lord with your whole heart. Proverbs 16:9 says: The heart of man plans his way but the Lord establishes his sleep. To receive what the Lord has already plan comes through being a doer of the

Word. A whole lot of people are one step from blessings, but they somehow get disconnected and want to do it themselves. In the Word of God, 1 Samuel 15th chapter, Saul was instructed to do something and turn out that he wanted to do it his way and not was instructed. Sometime are best thinking get us in shape we in. Sometimes that good feeling leads us to pits and prisons than palaces and promises. We miss the anointing because it looks or feels better to do it our way. But when you obey the Lord, that is when the glory comes, and the Lord is please. Always remember the devil will never agree to the word of the Lord. Satan is always at work trying to hinder, devour, detour and distract you from doing the Lord's will.

> Be sober, be vigilant; because your adversary the devil, as a roaring lion, walketh about, seeking whom he may devour.

(1st Peter 5:8)

The devil knows that there are great benefits in being obedient. He knows the closer you walk with the Lord the greater the blessings. He knows the more you seek the Lord, the more the anointing is going to live in you. The Lord promised the children of Israel that if they'd obey his commandments, they would live a blessed life in Canaan. Miriam's disobedience made the Lord angry and it caused them to be punished over and over and spend excessive years in the wilderness. We have to suffer to reign with the Lord. Romans 8:28 says: And we know that all things work together for good to them that love God and to them who are called according to his purpose. When we make wrong decisions, we are not aware or mindful of the consequences that come with disobedience,

because we get caught up in our feelings and flesh,

but when you are steadfast and unmovable,

blessings will start to manifest. Don't get caught up

in your flesh and become disobedient. Walk in the

way of the Lord.

Blessed is the man that walketh not in the counsel of the ungodly, nor standeth in the way of sinners, nor sitteth in the seat of the scornful.But his delight is in the law of the Lord; and in his law doth he meditate day and night.
And he shall be like a tree planted by the rivers of water, that bringeth forth, his fruit in his season; his leaf also shall not wither; and whatsoever he doeth shall prosper. The ungodly are not so: but are like the chaff which the wind driveth away. Therefore, the ungodly shall not stand in the judgment, nor sinners in the congregation of the righteous.
For the Lord knoweth the way of the righteous: but the way of the ungodly shall perish.
(Psalm 1)

Again, everything we need, all instructions and

directions are in the word of God. Continue to pray,

seek his face, and stay focus the word that will you daily. Praying will always be important with your walk with God. Prayer keeps you connected to the Lord and he will stay connected with you. We have read, studied, and heard down through the years, stories and testimonies of those that because of disobedience, either couldn't complete their assignments, or didn't receive their blessings. When we are disobedient, we lose, we come short of the promises, but when we are obedient and stand on his promises, we can receive continuously. Remember, if he said it, his word is his bond and that means he is obligated to bless your life.

> God is not a man, that he should lie; neither the son of man, that he should repent: hath he said, and shall he not do it? Or hath he spoken, and shall he not make it good?
> (Numbers 23:16)

So, if you are living in obedience expect what he has promised. Don't get discouraged if you can't see it, hold on, he will bring it to pass. Don't allow the opinion of others to distract you from the faith. If you are doing good and are rich, people are going to talk, if you are doing bad, and are poor, they are going to talk. I'd rather be on a stormy sea with the Lord, than on a peaceful shore with unbelievers. Make sure you are anchored in the Lord. What the Lord has for you is STRAIGHT OUTTA HIS HEART. Let the Lord be pleased with your obedience, so he will have the pleasure of blessing your life. Listen, you can always stand on the word of the Lord. His blessings are limitless, and he can do the impossible. There's no limit to what the Lord can do, nor any question that he can't answer. He is a miracle worker and he will never leave you nor forsake you. Always remember, his word stands.

> So shall my word be that goeth forth out of my mouth: it shall not return unto me void, but it shall accomplish that which I please, and it shall prosper I the thing whereto I sent it.
> (Isaiah 55:11)

> Delight thyself also in the Lord; and he shall give thee the desires of thine heart.
> (Psalm 37:4)

Before you petition the Lord about anything, know with confidence and great expectation that he knows what to do with your situation and he knows the answer and the solution. He wants us to trust him and walk in obedience. A lot of roads we travel are rocky, but he guides and leads us all the way. Roads of divorce, broken fellowship, the loss of a loved one, financial struggles, abuse, ridicule, and abandonment, but remember we serve a GOD that

What the Lord has for you is Straight Outta His Heart.

knows the road ahead. If he has called you to an assignment, he will escort you into victory. Not only will he lead you, but he will feed you with knowledge and understanding. In his presence is fullness of joy. YOU CAN HAVE THAT JOY!

One of the exciting things about the Lord blessing you is, if you stay obedient, there are countless blessings for your life. Keep praying and fasting, studying and abiding in his word and watch God do it, watch it come to past. He can reach the highest mountains, and he can reach in the lowest valleys. Even when you make a mistake, fall down, come short of, get up and dust yourself off, ask him to help you and he will. Stay in encouraged and mind the things of the Lord.

I'm so glad the perfect God took his perfect hand and laid it on an imperfect me. Give your life to him and become a Garment of Worship!

Moments of Reflection

YOU HAVE PURPOSE IN THIS LIFE…. Sometimes we are not aware of the call on our lives. Sometimes we have so many things that are going on that it can distract us from focusing on our God given assignment. The only sure way to know your purpose is to seek the Lord. Stay focused on his word. Learn how to fast and pray continuously. Remember, everything you need to survive is in the WORD OF GOD.

I pray that this journey in my life will not only help you but also encourage you to pursue and understand the calling in your life.

You can make it because the Lord will help you to take it.

"REMEMBER ONLY WHAT YOU DO FOR CHRIST WILL LAST

Leslie Wells

Leslie's Bio

Evangelist Wells is a native of Earle, Arkansas. Leslie is a long time member of the Church of God in Christ. She is married to Chane Wells, and has three children, Anthony, Christian and Ebonie. Evangelist Leslie Wells, values the work of the Lord. She accepted the Lord Jesus Christ as her personal Lord and savior and was Baptized the Holy Ghost on October 15, 1986.The foundation of Ministry in her life began its journey at the Earle Church of God in Christ in Earle, Arkansas. She was not only mentored by her pastor but also the mothers of the church. She is presently attending the Calvary Church of God in Christ. Evangelist Leslie Wells served on the West Memphis School Board and received the Master School Board Award. She attended Arkansas State University in Jonesboro, Arkansas, Mid-South Community College in West Memphis, Arkansas, Stratford Career Institute and The Agape Bible College where she was Ordained in Ministry in 2005. She also attended All Saints Bible College, as well as receiving her Evangelist Missionary License in 2012 from Tennessee 5th Jurisdiction. Evangelist Wells was appointed by Superintendent Nickols to serve in the Evangelism Department as Elect Lady in the C.C. Knox District. Evangelist Leslie Wells, in her life time in ministry, served as Assistant Superintendent of Sunday school, Youth President, President of Missionary Board, and Pastor's Aide.

Made in the USA
Middletown, DE
03 August 2021